Sherry & Sparkly

A Poetry Conversation

by

Maureen Cullen & Patricia M Osborne

Notes on the Poetry Conversation:

The idea behind the work is that it is a conversation in poetry between two poets. Each poem included is a reaction to what has come before.

The sequence starts with Maureen's 'Sister Song', which is followed by Patricia's 'Three in a Bed'. The poems alternate between the poets for the remainder of the conversation.

Contents

AUNTS AT HAVOC

The row descended
to the cliff edge at Havoc
where the Clyde
shimmered its way to the Firth,
eager for the sea.

I fidgeted as they trailed
the week's gossip between draws,
lipstick-smudged butts discarded
in the plant pot at the kerb,
two sisters gabbing for Alba.

They tipped it back like the water of life
as I frowned, weighed down
with small town spin,
wishing to sky-pedal with the geese,
over the river
out of this yard where the slope
was stayed with brick and hedge.

Decades later, the terrace clings on
while they both lie in Alcluith soil,
their gossip having mapped and recorded
a network of lives,
groundwork for a tide of kindnesses
both given and received.

ISOLATED

I'm the new kid, invisible
to the girls playing Two Balls
and long rope skipping
on the playground.

I wish I were back in Bolton sitting
close to my carrot-haired Susan.

At break time we'd wait
by the locked gate
for Senior boys
to pass us pear drops
through the black railings.

The bell on the puce wall vibrates,
children crowd into the building,
laughing and chatting. I follow,

shuffle round,
back and forth, late
for class, past
identical staircases,
toilets, cloakrooms, coats,
blue doors, yellow walls–

I reach a Post Office-like window,
            peep through the grille,

holding back.

'Please Miss, I'm lost.'

CHARLOTTE IN HER SUMMER DRESS

An August day, rationing relaxed,
a catalogue purchase to be paid in the year,
white cotton flare from a cinched-in waist,

tailored at the bust with two polo-mint buttons,
under a pale freckled décolletage,
eyes merry behind Sophia Loren glasses –

while a forest of fern, splayed like handprints,
swings free with the frock, a-swish in the breeze,
whenever she birls, and birls and birls.

VINYL HAIKU

Maggie May rotates
on my old record player.
I love Rod's spiked hair.

I dream every night
of T-Rex. Marc Bolan rides
his swan to Beltane.

David Cassidy,
breaking up is hard to do,
I think I love you.

On the octopus
like a spirit in the sky,
drunk from funfair dives.

AUTUMN FLOWER GIRL

I rush to the window in a sweep of silk
my wedding nails tap the glass

the limousine door inches ajar
her flower-girl dress floats like a bell

she stops her skip down our path
turns and raises her eggshell face

waves her freesia posy in trust
the door continues its shimmering arc

white bowed pumps scamper past
full of beginnings she dips her head

scrambles in, is swallowed up
by a final swing of October gold.

TEENAGE BRIDE

At Dad's side
I stroll down the aisle.

Husband to be,
turns to me.

We stand together,
vow to love forever.

The vicar speaks.
Don't laugh– breathe.

Confetti shaken,
photos taken.

Time to party,
sherry and sparkly.

MAKING DO

Edge out the deepest drawer
empty it of cloth and towel
chase rolling mothballs out
lay Grannie's muslin pouch aside
thumb all seams for skelf and nail
dampen your sponge
wipe each surface clean
line with well-napped boiled sheets
pack them thick, fold over
every rim, place it in a corner on the floor
select your softest blanket, pink
with satin trim, put it to your cheek, fold
and fold again to fit, turn it back

no need for cot or crib
palm space to slip her in.

NAPPY TIME

Sun-heat dries the whites
as they dance
on the whirligig
spinning in the breeze.

I fold a triangle, slip
the terry towel

under wriggling limbs,
wrap around. Fasten.

Screams from his cot urge
me to run and check–

Pin and skin intact.

MODERNITY

Perched on a high stool at my grille,
squeezed into stiletto heels,
I ink pounds and pence in passbooks,
thumb a thimble into sponge,
flick notes with the speed of a Las Vegas moll,
bundle pennies into hessian sacks to dump

in the walk-in safe, its shelves rich with crisp
wads of aromatic notes, the scent of money
beguiling as the oils in mahogany counters
and cigar smoke from gentlemen in pinstripe suits
who wait as I count, sift, stack and weigh
the stuff of my dreams. I'm on the top flight of modernity
with my Burroughs ABC, numbers flying

onto the roll as I type and lever. No need
to resort to that new computer, the size of four
washing machines, rumbling in a corner, displacing
two desks and three clerks, spoiling the effect
of Panama tobacco, brass-studded leather and dust.

CUT AND PASTE

'Just cut and paste,'
he shouts,
'press Control C– Control V.'

Busy making
gravy in the kitchen,
an image jumps
into my mind's eye–

a pair of scissors
cuts up screen images
and glues the pictures down.

I shake my head and laugh.

Cut and Paste stays a puzzle
until that special birthday gift

when my eleven-year-old teaches
me to type keyboard jargon into the PC.

HEGGIE'S BUILDING

Home was Heggie's Building,
up a charcoal close with spiral stairs,
like out a witch's tale. Don't ask me
who Heggie was. Some long dead
Glaswegian crook rubbing hands for rent.

We slept in the one room. Was bedlam
with the wean greeting and Da snoring
and, at night, boats bleating,
bringing bales of this and that to Port Glasgow
and earlier, drunks toasting themselves,
like princes, outside the County Pub.

I shut it out, holed up in my cabinet bed
living Sidney Carton's agonies –
It is a far, far better thing
that I do, than I have ever done –
courtesy of the lending library,
five more adventures lying flat
in the compartment over my head.
And if I was lucky, sucking Refreshers.

MILLENNIUM

Ice inside my bedroom window
vanished once central heating
shot the mercury sky-high.

Black and white televisions
with tiny screens projected
Dalek terror. We crept in twos
to the spooky backyard privy.

Curled up on the floor in PJs,
Mum brought us a cuppa
while we witnessed

Neil Armstrong bunny-hop
on the moon.

Transmission terminated,
buzzing drilled my consciousness.

We plugged in our first colour TV, switched
off the lights, rubbed hands, smiled–

watched with wonder,
hooked on Dallas and Dynasty.

A red telephone box at the corner of our street
left stranded – desecrated – vandalised–

replaced with a home phone
at the spin of a dial–

Mobiles to keep track of my young, angst
replaced ease when offspring ignored ringtones.

On the turn of the century, Big Ben chimed,
we linked arms to sing *Auld Lang Syne*,

chrysanthemums exploded in clouds
reflecting on The Thames,
London Eye illuminated spectrums of light
welcoming the arrival of the Millennium.

Acknowledgements from Maureen Cullen

Many thanks to the editor of Shooter in which the following poem was previously published:

Modernity   (2018) Issue 8 Summer 2018

Many thanks to Patricia M Osborne, Maggie Mackay, Trish McGrath, Corinne Lawrence, Sheena Bradley and Francesca Hunt for their continued support and guidance.

Acknowledgements from Patricia M Osborne

Many thanks to the editor of Impspired in which these poems have previously been published:

First Day at Juniors   (2020) Impspired Issue 7
Isolated   (2020) Impspired Issue 7
Millennium formerly TV Wonder   (2020) Impspired Issue 7

Special thanks to Maureen Cullen, Sheena Bradley, Corinne Lawrence, and Suzi Bamblett, for their continued support and valuable feedback.

Maureen Cullen and Patricia M Osborne would like to thank Mark Davidson at The Hedgehog Poetry Press for offering this publishing opportunity and being such an awesome editor to work with.

About Maureen Cullen

Maureen was born in West Dunbartonshire and now lives in Argyll and Bute. She is a retired social worker who specialised in fostering and adoption. In 2015, she gained an MA in Creative Writing from Lancaster University where she studied poetry and short fiction. She has been shortlisted in various competitions, including The Fish Short Story Prize and The Bristol Short Story Prize. In 2016, she was published by Nine Arches Press, along with three other poets, in *Primers 1*. She has poetry published in a range of magazines, including *Shooter* and *The Interpreter's House*. Her current project is a collection of linked short stories based in a fictional town in the West of Scotland.

About Patricia M Osborne

Patricia M Osborne is married with grown-up children and grandchildren and lives in West Sussex. In 2019 she graduated with an MA in Creative Writing. She is a published novelist, poet and short story writer. Her short stories and poems have been published in various literary magazines and anthologies and the final instalment of her *House of Grace* family saga trilogy was published March 2021. *Taxus Baccata* and *The Montefiore Bride* (Poetry pamphlets) were published by The Hedgehog Poetry Press 2020.

She has a successful blog at Whitewingsbooks.com where she features other writers and poets. When Patricia isn't working on her own writing, she enjoys sharing her knowledge, acting as a mentor to fellow writers. You can contact Patricia via the following medias: -

Facebook:	Patricia M Osborne, Writer @triciaosbornewriter
Website:	Whitewingsbooks.com
Twitter:	Patricia M Osborne @PMOsborneWriter